Breaking Ungodly

Soul Ties

Exposing the Enemy

By

PASTOR DEMOND L. TOLLIVER with Elise Shedd

Copyright © 2010 by Melchizedek Publishing

Book Cover Design and Printing: idg Company

Breaking Ungodly Soul Ties: Exposing the Enemy

ISBN 978-0-615-39130-4

All rights reserved. No part of this book may be reproduced, stored in a retrieval system, or transmitted in any form or by any means – electronic, mechanical, photocopy, recording, or any other—except for brief quotations in printed reviews, without the prior written consent of the publisher. If you purchase this book without a cover you should be aware that this book may have been stolen property and reported as "unsold and destroyed" to the Publisher. In such case neither the author nor the publisher has received any payment for this "stripped book."

Scripture quotations marked (AMP) are taken from the Amplified Bible, Copyright © 1954, 1958, 1962, 1964, 1965, 1987 by The Lockman Foundation. All rights reserved. Used by permission. (www.Lockman.org).

Scripture quotations marked (KJV) are taken from the Holy Bible, Copyright © 1973, 1978, 1984 by Biblica, Inc. ™ Used by permission of Zondervan. All rights reserved worldwide. www.zondervan.com

SPECIAL THANKS

This book is dedicated to God, My Beloved Mother, and

The Archbishop

John L. Lawson, Jr.

TABLE OF CONTENTS

INTRODUCTION

Many times in a Christian's walk, we become entangled and bound up by ties that become a stronghold in our lives. Strongholds can be anything hindering your walk with God or your pre-ordained destiny on earth. Sometimes, these strongholds can wrap tightly around your mind, body, soul, and spirit destroying you from the inside and out. Satan uses many devices and a snare to entangle the people of God for the simple assignment of taking you out of God's Will in your life and gets you off focus on the things of God. One of the many tactics Satan uses to rob us of our blessings is through ungodly soul ties. Ungodly soul ties are relationships unsanctioned by God or toxic in nature that can keep us in strongholds because of the people we are involved with. God desires for our soul and health to prosper living out our divine purpose in the earth so we must break any strongholds that hinder us especially the soul ties that bind us (**3rd John 2 KJV**).

Chapter 1: What Are Ungodly Soul Ties?

Ungodly soul ties can be any relationship between two people that develops into a stronghold that binds into their mind, body, soul and spirit. This relationship can be between men and women or the same-sex that is unsanctioned by God that results in spiritual bondage amongst the participators. In order to understand what ungodly soul ties are, it is important to know how God created us to operate in earthly and spiritual realms. In **1stThessalonians 5:23 (KJV)**, Paul exhorts the Body of Christ to allow "the very God of peace sanctify you wholly and I pray God your whole spirit and soul and body be preserved blameless unto the coming of our Lord Jesus Christ." Being made in the Image of God, God created us with a spirit because He is a spirit **(John 4:24 KJV)**. God operates in the spirit realm and needs a human vessel to work through to complete His Will in the Earth for the Body of Christ. Jesus became God in the flesh that houses His Spirit possessing a soul as well **(John 1:14; John 6:53 KJV)**. As humans who live in God's Earthly Kingdom, we have a body or earthsuit to live out our divine purpose in the physical realm also having a soul and spirit. The spirit or inner man dwells in our body but our soul is where our mind, will, and personality that makes us uniquely different from each other. Our souls were created to develop relationships that glorify the goodness and glory of God especially in the sanctity of the man-woman relationships leading to the godly celebration of marriage. God has given us free will to make choices in the earth including who we desire to marry in the earthly realms. In order for us to marry the person we desire, we have to follow out the Plan of God He has over our lives. When God created Adam, He saw that man shouldn't be alone and wanted to create a suitable creature or helpmeet that would fit into the original plan for Man so God didn't present Adam a helpmeet until he was complete in God and not lacking in any area. Adam allowed God to do a complete work in him by living out his divine purpose in the earth before receiving his mate to help him build up God's Kingdom in the earth. As Christians, we sometimes don't allow God to do a complete work in us to receive His Promises which may include a mate. As believers, we don't like to let patience have its perfect work by faithfully waiting on the manifestations of our heart's desire (**James 1: 2 KJV**). When we don't wait on God and try to create our own Ishmael blessings therefore breeding spiritual consequences because of our disobedience. This may ruin your relationships with people and God because of ill-gotten blessings. Adam and Eve were made and joined together by God in the sacredness of marriage but the relationship became strained when they were disobedient in the Garden of Eden which brought forth sin upon the earth. The act of sin marred and blemished godly relationships and since man has free will, he or she can develop ungodly soul ties to another person in hopes of possessing a mate.

Ungodly soul ties are relationships that seem to mirror the way we hope to bond with another person except it is deceptive in a nature for the people involved by developing a false sense of oneness. Any relationship between a man and woman that doesn't involve God or God didn't put together is doomed to fail and becomes toxic to your soul and spirit. Your soul has become bound around another's person's soul like an invisible chain that becomes stronger as you stay in that relationship becoming a stronghold allowing the spirit of bondage to dwell in your spirit.

Like a python, the doomed relationship squeezes the spirit man from hearing from God and keeps him or her from living out The Plan of God in their life. Satan uses these kinds of relationships to keep God's people from being truly effective in the Kingdom of God and win souls to Christ to develop into Disciples of Christ. The more bound you are to that person, the more the strongholds began to takeover or possess your entire being. If you continue to follow this path of destruction, you will become a reprobate vessel living completely outside the Will of God for your life eventually reverting back to a damned state destined for Hell. Ungodly soul ties can develop into living by the flesh and heeding to the carnal desires of the flesh **(Romans 8:15 KJV)**. Since man's fall from grace, man has the choice now to live for good or evil. He can serve God by developing his spirit man or serve his flesh living out every desire that isn't holy or beneficial to his destiny in life.

The Quest for Love: Premarital Sex

One of the major devices and snares Satan uses for mankind to develop ungodly soul ties is through the need for love. Everyone wants love, to be in love, and to have someone to love. Love isn't the same as lust but can intermingle within ungodly soul ties. Lust on its own involves a person just living to feel temporal pleasure confusing ecstasy with love. People dream of finding their true love or soul mate believing he or she will make their life complete. Stories, movies, and books are created to emphasize the burning need to have love. This burning need for love has been the downfall of many relationships even in biblical times. The need can become an all-consuming void in a person's life making him or her feel incomplete or unfulfilled in their earthly walk. They go on a desperate search for their true love sometimes compromising their moral values just to be with someone. A person meets a potential prospect in hopes that he or she is the one God created for him or her to become one in matrimony. Temptations arise when a person engages in pre-marital sex before marriage that starts the consequences of disobedience in the relationship. Pre-marital sex hinders the relationship from becoming what God desires it to be which is fulfilling, intimate, and mirrors our relationship with God Himself. The soul binds itself to the other person through pre-marital sex with Satan using this need to express physical love through evil manipulations so our flesh becomes defiled and craves more of this type of sin. Once our flesh becomes engage in this type of sin, it becomes harder to break loose from the continuous cycle of events that arises and destructive patterns develop as you become more unequally yoked **(Galatians 5:1 KJV)**. God warns us about becoming unequally yoked which means to not join with another person that God did not put into your life which can be friends and significant others. God has a distinct plan for our life which has wondrous things and blessings once we step on His Path of Ordered Steps in which He directs our ways of living in this earthly life. But if become bound and entangled in ungodly soul ties, we become like the person we are bound to in mind, body and soul **(1st Corinthians 6:15 KJV)**.

Destructive Consequences of Pre-marital Sex: Samson and Delilah

Starting in the book of Judges13, God rose up Samson to fight the Philistines and help to deliver God's people from the Philistines. Samson had supernatural strength from God to wage war on the Philistines but he loved him some girls which became his undoing. Samson develop his first ungodly soul ties when he married a Philistine woman who were the very people God was delivering His People from and didn't take heed to the warning signs of being unequally yoked. Samson was becoming a rebellious spirit and Satan began to use his weakness for women to eventually destroy him. We all have weaknesses that

Satan will exploit to usher our demise and stop the Plan of God in our lives. An ungodly soul tie is a very powerful weapon of the Enemy and Samson didn't realize that he had opened the door to Satan for his destruction. After marrying the Philistine woman, Samson began the cycle of committing adultery and fornication creating more ungodly soul ties in his destructive pathway. Delilah was being used by The Enemy to destroy Samson using the sin of pre-marital sex that he was already committing continuously releasing more demonic spirits to orchestrate his future death. When Samson fell in love with Delilah in Judges 16, he became infatuated with her by her seductive ability to entice men to do things they would not normally do.

In the midst of sleeping with harlots including Delilah, Samson wasn't listening or hearing from God to warn him of the consequences of sexual sin. Delilah had such a powerful seductive spirit that Samson became duped into revealing the source of his anointing and loss his anointing. His ungodly soul ties with Delilah cost him his anointing and his life in the end. God allowed Samson to use the anointing for the last time to destroy the Philistines in a building extinguishing his life as well.

You can lose your anointing by becoming bound to the wrong person and open the doors to the Enemy to attack your life or destroy your life. What Satan's goal is to derail God's plan for your life and for God to strip you of your anointing because of your disobedience.

Chapter 2: Who Are Your Ungodly Soul Ties?

Samson's ungodly soul ties started with a seed of rebellion by joining with women that God didn't place in his life for his ministry and destiny in life. Sometimes, our ungodly soul ties stem from rebelling against authority or someone warning us not to become involved with a particular person. If we disregard the warning signs, especially when God is telling is not to do it, then we step into a quicksand of disobedience that sinks us deeper into additional problem and painful consequences that might occur. In order to assess whether we are in an ungodly relationship, we need to identify and determine how this person is affecting our walk with God and daily lifestyle. If it is a godly relationship, it should only enhance your spiritual walk and make your life more fulfilling in every aspect. God wants us to have fulfillment not completion in another person and our relationships should add on to our sense of wholeness in ones' life. Ungodly soul ties can stem from this sense of incompletion or the need to have wholeness. The people we choose to develop relationships can make or break our destiny in God. Who are your ungodly soul ties and how did you become bound to him or her? What kind of factors and circumstances in your life that causes you to choose that particular person? Did you ask God whether this person should become part of your life or did you make the decision by yourself? These are questions you should be asking yourself if you are currently involved with someone and wonder if this person is what God brought into your life or not. Let's take a simple quiz to determine whether you are in an ungodly relationship or godly relationship.

What Kind of Relationship Are You In?

1. Is the person saved? Yes or No

2. Does the person regularly go to church? Yes or No

3. Is this person filled with the Holy Spirit? Yes or No

4. Are you engage in sexual activities with this person? Yes or No

If you answer yes to all or most of these questions, you aren't necessarily operating in a godly relationship. If you are continuing in this type of relationship, answer the next series of questions.

What Kind of Ungodly Soul Ties Are You In?

1. Have you asked God about whether this person is the one for you? Yes or No

2. If God said no this is not the person, are you still keeping in contact with this person? Yes or No

3. Has your relationship with this person become obsessive? Yes or No

4. Are you thinking about this person all the time in your daily living? Yes or No

5. Does it feel like you want to give your all to this person no matter what? Yes or No

6. Are you beginning to compromise your beliefs and do things because you are so in love with this person? Yes or No

7. Are you making excuses for this person's questionable actions done to you or others? Yes or No

8. Is it getting harder to hear from God or listen to other people who are worried about your relationship with this person? Yes or No

9. **Are you offended or defensive when someone talks about that person? Yes or No**

10. **Does your mind feel cluttered or hard to concentrate on the simplest of things such as praying or talking to God? Yes or No**

If you answered yes to any of these questions then you are walking on dangerous ground. These kinds of soul ties are like a minefield in which it is only a matter of time when something will explode and implode destructively in your life with spiritual and natural consequences.

The famous answer that people give when they are in a blooming relationship is that God sent this man or woman into my life and we are so happy in love. Unfortunately, we don't know how happy or unhappy in love these people are truly in. People love to say that God told them that "This is the person I am supposed to be with or that person told him or her that God meant for us to be together." If you answered yes to the first question on whether you asked God about this person instead of no, then you are either in denial or blind to the signs of ungodly soul ties. If you answered no, then you are well on your way to breaking ungodly soul ties and the strongholds that are part of this type of hindrance to our spiritual walk.

Did You Ask God To Be With This Person?

Those who are ready to know what makes up ungodly soul ties should have truthfully asked this important question. People that walk into our lives can be just passing through and shouldn't be given a permanent status. Godly relationships that God put together don't involve pre-marital sex nor tears you away from participating in the things of God. No person should take priority or precedent over what God has for you and wants for you to do. A lot of heartache and pain could be prevented if we just asked God whether this person is beneficial or hindrance to my life. God wants to be part of every aspect of your life including who you choose as a soul mate. There are many people who wish they had never met so and so with much regret. It becomes a problem expounded when children are part of your ungodly soul ties and can be the tragic casualties of this toxic relationship. Our choices don't affect just our lives but those around us. Becoming tied to the wrong person is like an invasion of the soul snatchers. Once you allow a person to invade your soul twisting you mentally, physically, and spiritually, then you begin to be taken over in every way until you literally bound to that person with your whole being. If you are engaged in pre-marital sex, then you are spiritually bound to that person leading to ungodly actions to maintain your bound status with this person. That person becomes a stronghold and bondage that keeps you from being free to serve God and His People with all of your heart and soul. Since God is a jealous

God, He doesn't condone any relationship that overtakes His Relationship with you. So if God said no and you didn't heed the answer, then you are on your own and will find out what happens when we are disobedience to God's directions.

I Was Lonely, God

The spirit of loneliness is the major reason why people develop ungodly soul ties. A person who has a lonely spirit thinks that he or she is all by themselves not realizing that the Holy Spirit is there as a Comforter for times such as these. To accept loneliness is a choice and can be an excuse to find oneself in an ungodly relationship to appease this spirit. The reason or explanation we give to God on why we are now in bondage with another person is because we were so lonely. But, God, I was so lonely and needed someone to talk to. The need for companionship is a desire not a need for God always reminds us that we are never alone in this earth. You can be with someone and still be lonely because he or she weren't meant to provide everything you need. There are married people right now that have feelings of loneliness sharing a bed with another person. The Enemy will use the spirit of loneliness to get you to operate in ungodly soul ties through feelings of desperation and despair. We get hooked up with the wrong person and the feelings of loneliness become even more so. Being single has been warped by the world's view in that everybody who is single is just waiting for the right person to come along.

The single person in the world is someone incomplete until they find the person who will make them complete and whole. This is not God's view on singleness which neither feeds on the mindset negative nor designed to make a person feel like their life isn't fulfilled without another person in it. Singleness is a state that a person goes through to live out their creative purpose and following God's Will or Plan for his or her life. A person who is single is developing completion and wholeness in every area of his or her life by allowing God to change them from the inside out. Once the person has maximized their single state, then they are ready for the next state which is the courtship and married state. Being single is not the end of the world for you and God isn't denying you the desire to be married but everything has a season and time **(Ecclesiastes 3:1-8 KJV)**. If we aren't careful, we will create our Ishmael blessings causing more problems in the long run when we pair up with the wrong person. Becoming lonely and impatient brings about a relationship that can bring more loneliness, pain, and other binding spirits to maintain it by any means necessary. The more we try to keep ungodly soul ties, the more spirits began to come into your life not including the spirits that the person may possess as well. Once you bind to another person, you partake in whatever spirits they have as well which makes you even more imprisoned spiritually, physically, and mentally.

The Ladies of Solomon

Solomon was a great king who asked God for wisdom and he was known throughout the lands for his riches and kingdom. Even the Queen of Sheba had to visit him to see how great King Solomon was. Solomon had been told by God not marry women of particular cultures and religions to maintain the purity of the kingdom to avoid idol worshipping. He didn't heed to God's instructions and began to marry other wives who came from idol religions developing a multitude of ungodly soul ties. Solomon had so many ladies that were ungodly soul ties that their idols and religion began to warp his mind into making idol statutes blatantly allowing the ladies to worship their own gods. As a result, Solomon became miserable, confused, vexed in the spirit being God-inspired to write a book in the bible called Ecclesiastes lamenting his selfish ways. When Solomon developed ungodly soul ties with various women, he opens the door to more unclean spirits to dwell in his earthly temple diminishing his great wisdom and anointing. Your earthly temple houses God's spirit but when you become bound to another person in an ungodly relationship that involves pre-marital sex, your temple invites unclean spirits to dwell pushing out the Holy Spirit. God's spirit cannot dwell in an unclean temple and you began to house additional spirits that are hell-bent on keeping you in bondage with that person.

Chapter 3: The Effects of Ungodly Soul Ties: David and Bathsheba

The effect of ungodly soul ties not only affects the person involved, but also the people that surround these types of relationships. Sometimes, we are not where we are suppose to be in the things of God and wind up in a place where Satan uses a satanic decoy to derail us from God's Plan in our life. Satan's purpose is to destroy your life, your ministry, and the next generation of people who are depending on your obedience to the Will of God. Your family will reap disobedient actions from generations to come activating the consequences that are devastating because you void the Blessings of Abraham and the inheritance God put into your life to possess in this earth. King David was a man after God's Own Heart and worshipped God in psalms and praises, but he allowed himself to not be on his God-given assignment leaving a door open for Satan to use his eyes to tempt him into sin, death, and future consequences of his actions. Satan knows that men are visual creatures and admire the physical attributes of a woman. He knew that King David loved women in general for having so many wives and concubines already in his possession. So when David gazed upon

Bathsheba bathing, his eyes developed lust in them which was the beginning of the sin that escalated to adultery and murder through this ungodly soul tie. David lusted and wanted Bathsheba so much that he had her husband killed in battle just to possess her. He even took blatant step of marrying Bathsheba and was going to continue on this road of destructive patterns until God sends a prophet rebuked of his great sin. King David repented to God but the repercussions of his sin became part of his family curse and caused more tragedies to occur in the next generation. Ungodly soul ties can bring about familiar spirits that can latch onto to your family and cause additional curses to be brought upon you causing generational curses. From his act of adultery, lust, and murder, these spirits became part of his family line and sadly, David was able to witness the affects of his decision to have Bathsheba at all costs. The generational curses continued onto King David's children especially with the spirits of lust, obsession, and infatuation. These spirits became a catalyst of more pain and sorrow for King David who was reaping the seed of disobedience and rebellion that is upon his family.

Obsession, Infatuation, and Lust

King David was obsessed with Bathsheba and committed murder to have her. As a result, King David's son, Amnon, had the spirit of lust that fell upon him when he became obsessed with his own sister Tamara. Amnon became so infatuated with his sister that he used trickery and lies to rape his sister Tamara developing a hatred for her afterwards. In the bible Amnon loved Tamara, but actually it was more like infatuation for once he possessed what he desired, he didn't want her anymore. Of course, the story became even worse with Amnon's brother Absalom killing him because of raping his sister Tamara after defiling her in a most shameful matter. This all stemmed from King David's actions of long ago and the same spirits came upon his own children sorrowfully.

When we embark in an ungodly relationship, we open the doors of rebellion and for Satan to bring more of his spirits to maintain the toxicity of the relationship or simply keep you miserably together by any means necessary. Obsession can play a crucial part in maintaining an ungodly soul tie with a person in that it can rob you of thinking clearly and decision-making becomes cloudy in every area of your life. When you devote your entire being to another person, it squeezes out the God-factor in your life because He has been replaced by your significant other. You begin to just think, breathe, walk, work, and talk about this person in your everyday life. God wants to be part of every facet of your life and ungodly soul ties causes us to ignore His Presence by elevating a person to become a false god in a sense that he or she is your everything. Your belief that this is real love when it's actual infatuation fuels the actions you take to keep the relationship going no matter how destructive it becomes to your well-being and those around you. It becomes a sickness that taints and affects your mind, body, and soul that can literally kill you if you continue to subject yourself to this kind of relationship. People have tendency to put another person on a pedestal and literally worship the ground he or she walks on which isn't fair to the person and to God. God warns us about putting anything before him which is a form of rebellion and an act of disobedience. If we continue in the relationship, God will allow the consequences of our actions rob us of our joy, peace, faith, and blessings that He desires for us to have. Satan enjoys when we are rebellious to God's Way of developing godly relationships and knows this a weapon that has destroyed marriages, ministries, and lives as well.

The Ultimate Goal of Satan's Use of Ungodly Soul Ties

Satan desires to kill, steal, and destroy all of God's people through his tactic of people developing ungodly soul ties. His goal is to kill the plan of God in that person's life, steal their blessings that are due to that person, and destroy their life which is the ultimate goal for Satan. The spirits that are tied to ungodly soul ties are the obsessive spirit, the lustful spirit, and the spirit of murder. When a person gets to the point in the ungodly relationship in which their mind is completely destroyed, their soul is bombarded by countless spirits, and their spirit is dead to hearing from God. That is when Satan begins his mission to kill the person entirely and he wants to destroy both of the people in the relationship. Just like the calico cat and dog story, Satan wants you and your partner to rip each other apart until you become reprobate creatures of carnality and iniquity. The effects of ungodly soul ties can lead to additional mayhem, more destructive patterns, and escalated chaos in your life. Everything that can go wrong does because The Enemy continues to attack your life in every direction because you are open to his other evil minions to attack you even more. Total possession can occur in your total being by your soul ties with another person and make your mind controlled by evil spirits. Now, Satan has full reign to throw fiery darts that can't be quenched since God's Spirit has left you. The Holy Spirit cannot dwell in our unclean spirits especially when we are in a harlot state.

God reminds us in His Word that, "Know ye not that your bodies are the members of Christ? shall I then take the members of Christ, and make them members of a harlot? God forbid." **(I Corinthians 6:15 KJV)**. Once you join your flesh to another person for fornication, you become joined to that person or harlot in God's eyes. **(I Corinthians 6: 16 KJV)**. Your body is the temple of the Holy Spirit and the more you engage in unsanctioned relationships, He disengages Himself from your temple. When we continuously sin, the Holy Spirit leaves us because He is grieved and vexed by the transgressions you keep committing repeatedly. The tragic repercussions of ungodly soul ties sears the conscience of that person allowing The Enemy to use you completely for his purpose of total destruction

(Romans 1:28 KJV). You are now a willing vessel for The Enemy to use in the earth realm to do his bidding because you have given the Devil place or an opportunity to wreak havoc in your life **(Ephesians 4:27 KJV).** Your ungodly relationships have allowed him to use any measures to maintain your warped sense of love to that person. This person is being used as well for The Enemy's devices of cutting you completely from The Will of God in your life. You start to think of dire actions to keep this person in your life or just prevent that person from leaving altogether. The spirit of suicide, murder, and death are the main culprits that aid in orchestrating destruction in your life.

Chapter 4: The Enemy's Use of Ungodly Soul Ties

The purpose of Satan's use of ungodly soul ties is to unleash the demons of murder and death into the earthly realms. His goal is to claim territory of every place in the world unleashing these demons upon God's people especially in these last days. The Devil wants to kill every human being he possibly can before The Return of Jesus. The relationship area in humans tends to be the weapon Satan uses to gain a foothold of attacking families, ministries, and people in authority by planting these demons of mass destruction. Be careful of the company you keep has a greater weight in what you surround yourself is what you will ultimately become. If you are in a godly relationship, you stay godly, holy and accountable to God. If you are in an ungodly relationship, you become a demonic pawn developing a more intense sinful nature, unrepented and even more carnal acting. You may get to the point where you may want to take another person's life or hurt the person in a physical, abusive matter in order to keep control over the relationship alive, dead, or badly maimed. In every sin committed, death occurs spiritually and transfer itself to the physical bringeth forth physical death if allowed to mature fully (**James 1:15 KJV**). The more you sin, the more you physically, spiritually, and emotionally die until you are operating on the unction of the evil spirits that now are housed in your defiled temple. The evil spirits seduce you into thinking that he or she is the only person for you and that you need to do whatever it takes to keep the love alive. As a result, confusion arises with suicidal thoughts and you begin to contemplate methods of maintaining the toxic relationships by any unnatural, ungodly means that destroys the God part of your human spirit. Then the flesh has full reign subjecting you to endure pain, torment, temporal pleasure, and fleeting emotions of infatuation mixed with lust. The more you allow yourself to endure such turmoil is like entering the boxing ring defenseless with no gloves and no muscle power. The opponent boxer keeps hitting and knocking you out, beating you down, and keep you crazily getting up to endure additional blows of suffering. It will eventually TKO your praise, your prayer, your anointing, and your power from God. God warns us to not be unequally yoked nor have any alliance with people inconsistent with your faith **(II Corinthians 6:14 KJV)**. We are not to fraternize with people who are involved in iniquities and a transgression for this unequal yoking becomes a constricting rope that gets tighter in its hold on people. Throughout the Word of God, when God put two people together, it was for the vision of God, the purpose of God, and for the edification of The Body of Christ. We forfeit our blessings and favor of God when we decide to put ourselves together with another person who is not what God has chosen for us to bond with.

What about the Kids God?

God's people can be destroyed by a lack of knowledge when it comes to making decisions that affect our futures and destinies in life **(Hosea 4:6 KJV)**. For various reasons such as becoming weary in waiting on God, constant setbacks and delays, and feelings of loneliness that we take on illegal love affairs doing everything married couples do sometimes bringing children in the relationship. Children are gifts from God and their spirits are planned in the heavenly realms pre-ordained and predestined before birth. But, if things are done in decency and in order, then there are less problems and challenges to rectify being out of order especially when it comes to having children. But there's a matter of ill-timing on us when we bring children into ungodly soul ties. The children may witness and endure the toxicity and negativity of the relationship. The children may begin to suffer the same spiritual poisonings as you do and The Enemy can bring attacks upon them at an early age. There's no hedge of protection amongst children who are subjected to the spirits that flood your unholy alliance with another person. Whatever comes upon you and your partner, those spirits can house in your children causing a generational curse to affect your family line in the future. If the Devil can destroy the next generation with family curses, then he will if allowed entry within ungodly relationships.

Ungodly Courtships and Shacking

Since you continue to flaunt your iniquitous unity, you desire now to make your relationship truly unofficial in the God's eyes by dwelling in the same abode giving evil spirits a feeding ground to make you and your partner miserable. But you plan to marry someday and eventually have a Bridezilla or Groomzilla wedding in the future. First, let's practice the married life including the bed as well. God will judge those who dishonor the marriage bed by participating in any sexual vices and fornication. In **Hebrews 13:4 KJV,** The Word says that, "Marriage is honourable in all, and the bed undefiled: but whoremongers and adulterers God will judge." Ungodly courtships and shacking involve of course pre-marital sex, raising possible bastards in the process, and trying to make your make-shift matrimonial life work. God never put in His bible to test the marriage bed out before marrying. Paul speaks in 1st Corinthians that for a man to "avoid fornication, let every man have his own wife, and let every woman have her own husband." (**I Corinthians 7:2 KJV**). God tells a man to not touch an unmarried woman or cohabitate with her for the reason that it causes chains of events in people's lives that causes more heartache and problems especially during break-ups. Tasting the forbidden fruit of the marriage bed makes the relationship has more strongholds to set in and make the soul ties even harder to unwind from so easily. In the beginning of the bible, Adam and Eve partook of the forbidden fruit to posses the knowledge of good and evil and this act of disobedience made their lives harder and less bountiful causing their offspring to be partakers of rebellion and sin. Co-habitation aka shacking brings forth a legal marriage license excluding God in the mix and now you have ungodly legally bound soul ties. And once you get a ring on it, it doesn't clean up the mess nor make the bow on an opened before marriage present any sweeter or precious. The simple fact of the matter, you got hitched, that's it.

The Plagues of Ungodly Soul Ties

A sickness comes into the soul that permeates through the physical body with every sinful action committed. There's a sickness in the mind that causes mental instability with a development of an unsound mind finding you on the verge of insanity. Sickness can enter your soul changing your very personality making your behaviors and actions the complete opposite of who you really are. Your behaviors become anti-Christ in nature and you begin to do unmentionable things that are shocking to the people around you. Once the sickness takes over your mind and soul, it may manifest itself into a physical disease of sorts that begins to hurt, and create pain that can destroy your earthly vessel. Satan uses sickness as a form of attacks by killing the physical body slowly and extinguishing the life of that person to destroy his or her divine purpose in the earth. Your heart dictates the health of your body spiritually and physically. Heart diseases and other illnesses can be a result of ungodly soul ties that break down the physical body from the countless attacks of The Enemy. Many of the diseases of today sometimes are consequential leading to untimely deaths in the Earth such as AIDS that came as a result of the transgressions of mankind in embarking on ungodly partnerships even with the same sex. Satan runs to and fro seeking willing participants in ungodly soul ties developing a binding relationship until death parts you both in more ways than one. That allows you to receive curses upon curses following sickness, pain, and possibly death. And if Satan can get you into Hell and dead early, so be it.

Chapter 5: How Do I Break Ungodly Soul Ties?

The Fallout

Just like vines that become entangled around a house becoming intertwined and twisted as it grows, your ungodly soul ties have the same effect. If you are in a relationship of this nature, it is time to evaluate and determine the cost of your soul to keep this love alive. Seeking God on this matter can liberate you and give you the courage to break ungodly soul ties the right way allowing restoration to take place. There's nuclear fallout that occurs after you have broken ungodly soul ties that can make you or break you. Some people break up because of various reasons besides a revelation from God but continuously deal with the aftermath effects that have toxified the mind, body, and soul. They may not be bound physically with that person anymore but they are still in bondage for what has entered their temples spiritually and emotionally. The recovery process takes time with God and learning how to use The Word of God to rebuild your faith in God's Plan in your life. In the book of Hosea, God says that "My People perish from a lack of knowledge" and God's people perish after involving themselves in soul ties and breaking these ties without God's restoration. (**Hosea 4:6 KJV**). Without the proper recovery from God concerning ungodly soul ties, the person can become their own worst enemy blocking his or her own recovery because of the strongholds. Strongholds keep a person in the same mindset and behaviors that strangle the liberating life that God has for us. You are literally imprisoned by strongholds with unclean spirits becoming emotionally disturbed in which your body was constantly fed with repeatedly by bonding with the other person. Once you stop the feeding of your transferred transgressions, you are left tormented and hungry for the next replacement to feed your iniquitous cravings. This begins a cycle of finding more ungodly soul ties because your spirit attracts the same kind of familiar spirits to keep you in more bondage.

The Cycle of Ungodly Soul Ties

You live and die by the choices you make in the earth **(Proverbs 18:21 KJV)**. The choices to go into more ungodly soul ties will only escalate into a possible miserable existence and an untimely death. Instead of another relationship, you may use other substitutes to heal your broken heart like a form of substance just to keep you going such as alcohol and drugs. You may take random multiple partners to ease your lustful needs but go back home wailing like a jilted lover. Depression may set in where you are taking pills to keep you in a good mood until they wear off allowing the tormenting spirits to bring you further down in sorrow and heartache. Sadly, some people never fully recover from ungodly soul ties because of suicide in that they are unable to live without that person in life. Making this person into a god or idol for devotion and earthly worship has caused you to eventually want to lash out in hurt, rage or despair. This can lead to pre-meditated murders and vengeful deaths by lovers scorned which has been the topic of many true crimes cases in the world. The cycle of ungodly soul ties ushers in the possibility of abusing other people physically and emotionally because of your pain in which the casualties may involve the children. It takes literally an act of God to fully break free from ungodly soul ties.

I Can't Eat nor Sleep

Your heart hurts at the thought of no longer being with that person. You function at about 50% of your true self living daily barely. Food has become a past occurrence because your sorrow has robbed you of an appetite. You have such heartache for this person wondering what went wrong and if you had to do it all over again. This is where your find yourself in a dark place and at a cross roads as well. This is when you have to make a conscious decision to break ungodly soul ties from your mind, body, and soul through spiritual means. You have to take back your spirit man from The Enemy in order to have your mind and soul back. It's going to take spiritual warfare for you to reclaim your holy vessel and bring it back into the Presence of God. But, Satan isn't going to let you go so easily without a fight and will use more attacks against you to keep you going downhill for the goal of self-destruction. To be free completely, it's going to take God's power, God's Word and His Anointing to fight the Devil. **(Ephesians 6:12 KJV)**.

Relapse

We do fall back into these ungodly relationships sometimes because we haven't found God's Way or another positive option to become completely liberated from that person. This isn't the time to blame neither yourself nor feel sorry for yourself because of sinning again because you fell for the "I'm sorry or Can we try again?" You must remember that your will is probably still connected to that person and still needs the power of God to break the soul ties. The thing that has to happen is to repent to God and strive to live out God's plan in His Word and self-discovery. Repentance comes with admittance of our sins and asking God to forgive us of our sins. The most important part of breaking ungodly soul ties is to admit you made a mistake in your partner choice and repenting to God. The next thing is to forgive the person so you will not become bitter and resentful harboring past hurt for years at a time. Unforgiveness robs you of living a fulfilled life and can manifest itself in sicknesses and diseases. God wants you to forgive yourself and that person which is the beginning of the liberation process **(Luke 6:37 KJV)**.

Don't Look Back

In Genesis 19, Lot's wife glanced back at the destruction of Sodom and Gomorrah becoming a pillar of salt by God. Apparently, Lot's wife had some unholy regrets and possibly some unholy soul ties in this wicked city. Sodom and Gomorrah was a city in biblical times where the city inhabitants were so wicked and deep in sexual sin committing other forms of debaucheries that God sentenced them to death. The people had such reprobated, carnal minds that God's wrath destroyed the entire city leaving no trace of its existence. Lot's wife fell to the same judgment by God when she looked back at the evil place when God instructed them not to look back. If you choose to look back at your past relationship with regrets and remorse, your journey to freedom will be halted and may revert back to the same bad habits before. In your journey to break free from ungodly soul ties, you can't afford to look back and regret leaving the situation. The worst decision you can make is to return from the sinful behavior in which you were delivered from. Residuals of old mental thought patterns and behavior from ungodly relationships are natural through the recovery process and you will be under attack by The Enemy to resume the self destructive behaviors with that person. The Enemy will even use that person as a deceiver of sorts to keep you constantly distracted and holding on to some hope of reconciliation. Yes, you will feel despair, loneliness, and confusion but worst things can come your way if you return back to that toxic relationship where there maybe no point of return. Before you think to resume the relationship again, seek God's wisdom on the matter and pray for the strength to endure the sufferings that comes from breaking your soul ties.

But, They Can Change God

Yes, God can change a person if that person desires change but that doesn't mean that he or she is the chosen vessel for covenant partnership in the form of marriage. God can't go against free will in man nor make someone love you nor be with you. Once you get the revelation that the relationship was doing more harm than good in terms of your destiny and purpose in life, the person doesn't fit into neither the equation nor the Plan of God in your life. God can then help you remove the negative feelings and emotional rollercoaster of loving the wrong person that is hindering the blessings God wants to bring into your life.

Chapter 6: Fasting and Prayer Breaks Ungodly Soul Ties

Your mind, body, and soul have been in the war zone of toxic love and what has suffered has been your spirit man. Your spirit man no longer has the Holy Spirit speaking to it because of the many spirits housed in your temple, due to ungodly soul ties. You function without God's power so things that occur in your life upset you more and offend you more. It's hard to get things to work on your behalf because your prayer life is dead or non-existent. It's difficult to give God the praise because your spirit is filled with junk, uncleanness, and unforgiveness. An ungodly relationship affects your entire existence so don't be surprised when your temple is in spiritual and physical turmoil making you moody and mean all the time. All the crying in the world isn't helping you release the spirits that are still tormenting your mind repeatedly, over past failures and past relationships. Flesh has had full reign in your life so the first thing that you need to do is put the flesh under submission **(Romans 8:4-7 KJV)**. The flesh wants to control your life and keep you carnal minded. Developing ungodly soul ties gave the flesh a grand opportunity to have what it wanted no matter how or when it gets it. Living by the flesh leads to death spiritually and physically but God wants you to live by His Spirit in which He reveals the spiritual truths that lead to victorious living **(Galatians 5:16 KJV)**.Since your unholy bond with another person has infected your life like a cancer eating away at your temple, it's going to take fasting and prayer to break the chains of ungodly soul ties **(Mark 9:29 KJV)**.

Fasting and Prayer

Fasting is a spiritual and physical action that can make your temple more submissive to God's spirit. It allows God to purge and rid your spirit man of unclean spirits along with any other issues you have in your life. The purging process takes time for God has to literally clean your temple of the junk and mess your spirit man endured because of your spiritual connection with another person. Ungodly soul ties corrupt your spirit man wreaking chaos in your soulish area. Your soulish area has damaging deposits of repeated attacks from the spiritual realm by The Enemy. Fasting helps to get the flesh under control so it doesn't dictate your whims, such as listening to your ex profess his or her undying love for you and being seduced by lustful temptations. The act of fasting is more than just not eating but a spiritual weapon against the lusts of our flesh and allows us to return to praying more effectively. It takes fasting and praying on a consistent basis to become free from ungodly soul ties. Prayer keeps you in constant communication with God who will help you renew your mind to His Word and change your thought patterns of being obsessed and infatuated by this person.

Dying To Self for God

In order for God to do a good work the supernatural way, your fleshly way of having a relationship with a person has to die in the process. The flesh lives to do whatever it wants to do regardless of the consequences. Your flesh was the driving force of the relationship by dominating your choices and decision making in life. God needs to take your flesh out of the equation for His Spirit to dwell in you once more. Your flesh is going to continually fight you for the rest of your days but doesn't have to dictate your every day life. Once you allow God to work on your temple through fasting and prayer, the restoration process can truly begin. When you don't feed the flesh with food, you open the door for God's Power to bring true deliverance from ungodly soul ties in your life. Now, the Holy Spirit can help you into creating new behaviors of holiness and godliness becoming less enslaved by strongholds and relationship bondages. But total freedom from this bondage is going to take more than just going to church and laying of hands to reach total deliverance. It is now time for you to develop a godly relationship with The Most High to help you see what love truly is.

Chapter 7: Developing a Personal Relationship with God

When we love another person, we are blind to their true intentions and hidden motives so self denial sets in on truly what we feel. We are blind to the false sense of love thinking that this twisted infatuation is true love. Once you have broken your emotional soul ties with him or her, you can begin to learn how to love the way God loves and know how biblical love is. For with God's love come joy, peace and fulfillment in life to overcome trials and tribulations in every part of our existence. The world's definition of love has conditions and relies on the reciprocity of the other person. Love in man's eyes is "I will love you if you love me" mentality. We call this kind of love "fleeting love" in which your moods dictate how much in love you are at a given time. It is also based on the feelings of happiness which changes based on your situation and has no relation to joy. Joy sustains you regardless of how you feel because it is God providing rest within your spirit to withstand situations in your life that comes your way. The love that God desires for us to experience comes from developing a personal relationship with God. In order for you to be able to love a person unconditionally, you need to experience true love in God. People love to recall their first loves and rehash the fond memories of that time continuing to seek a second, third, and fourth love creating more bad memories that don't help you form the true relationship with God. But truly, your first love should be Jesus making Him Lord over your life. Once you get saved, your life isn't your own to do what you want to do **(Romans 10:9 KJV)**. God has now become the Lord over your life and has the final say on what you do in your life if you allow Him to. God desires for you to abide in His Presence as He Abides in You **(John 15:4 KJV)**.The more you stay in the Presence of God, the more of His Love He showers upon your spirit man until it overflows in every facet of your life. God's love is never ending and never-ceasing and once you experience it in your daily walk with Him, it begins to become part of who you are and how you treat other people. Every person that you encounter should see and receive the overflow of God's love in you including your future husband and wife. God love us unconditionally in spite of our flaws and faults. You also have The Holy Spirit who is also your Comforter in times of loneliness and pining for no-good false soulmates. There are people who allege they are Christians but they never develop a personal relationship with God yet want The Blessings to chase them down. To know God is to seek God's Kingdom and His ways of living righteously **(Matthew 6:33 KJV)**. Then when you delight yourself in the Lord, He will truly give you your heart's desire which may include a mate **(Psalms 37:4 KJV)**. The problem occurs when we decide to seek the add-to blessings without knowing God first.

My First Love

King David had a deep relationship with God in such a profound way that he wrote a book of psalms expressing his love for God in spite of his faults, flaws and the murder that he committed. King David was a man truly in love with God and God's love helped him even in the worst of times in his life. God's consuming love keeps you grounded especially in breaking ungodly soul ties and recovering from the damage caused by these unholy ties. When you make God truly your first love, it becomes easy to not fall to the snares of The Enemy who wants you to recall your past relationships that failed and how you are never going to find the one God has for you. The Enemy doesn't let up when you decide to pursue the things of God and will throw every fiery dart in your mind to resurrect a past flame in order to make you go back to your broken soul ties. God has to become your everything in every way to keep you anchored in His Word and His Presence in your life. God is a jealous God and knows if you harbor anything else besides Him in your heart especially another person, your heart suffers. There is a place in your heart that only God can fill and make whole, that anything else you put in there will have counterfeit effects. Your ungodly soul ties seem like it was fulfilling what your heart desires but your heart stills yearn for the love which is the agape love that is unconditional and never ends. Your ungodly soul ties were conditional in nature and depended on your emotional ties with that person. You felt so happy and alive when you were with that person and then the next time you felt so confused and hurt at what that person did to you calling this unconditional love. God has a definition in His Word about what love truly is and how as a person we are to walk in love. In **1st Corinthians 13:13**, God defines in His Word that "Love is patient, love is kind. It does not envy, it does not boast, it is not proud. It is not rude, it is not self-seeking, it is not easily angered, and it keeps no record of wrongs. Love does not delight in evil but rejoices with the truth. It always protects, always trust, always hopes, always perseveres" (**KJV**). This is what unconditional love truly is and your ungodly soul ties probably did not match in this definition being the complete opposite of love. Love is an action that is demonstrated in how we conduct our behavior and the person you were with probably showed you a false belief that it was love based on physical actions. False love can seem like true love when that person is talking to you nicely, treating you well, and seem to love the Lord appearing to have it all together or so it seems. But, true love stands the test of trials, tribulations, weight gain, pain, death, sorrow, and anything that may come against you in this life. False love may leave you when you no longer look attractive, may become bored with you, a crisis occurs showing you this isn't the right relationship to be in, or simply he or she wants to be with someone else. Whatever the reason it may be, that isn't love and this is when we become heartbroken in that we thought we truly loved this person with our whole-being not realizing that God is the only one that deserves that kind of love. God knows how to maximize the love factor in which it begins to encompass your entire being. God is love and when we compare His Love to your ungodly soul ties' love, it doesn't even come close to it because nothing God brings into your life should cause sorrow. If that person brought nothing but suffering and sorrow in most of the relationship, then you weren't in a loving relationship. A loving relationship with God gets better over time and makes you stronger in your faith walk in living out your divine purpose. You are safe in His Arms when you love on Him which makes you feel the love that you were trying to find in your ungodly soul ties. But, how do I begin to experience this kind of love with God to keep me from falling for the same relationship patterns with other people? How do I maintain my focus on developing my relationship with God and not get distracted by my senses especially with the opposite sex? In order to answer these questions, you must realize there are many things you must do spiritually in order to experience God's Love and have the ability to love others the way He loves you. Jesus made this His greatest commandment to love one another in God's way not man's way because it destroys the spirit of offense from setting in when people fall short of the glory of God. We are not perfect but God continues His Work in us daily and love keeps us from making judgments, having unforgiveness in our hearts, and striking the other cheek when we really want to.

Get Into His Word

In order to know God truly, you have to get into His Word and learn how God operates in the earth on your behalf in life. Whatever you desire or need from God can be found in His Word which has just about every answer or solution to the problems you experience in this earthly life. To see how much love a person can have for God, reading the book of Psalms gives you pause on how intimate your relationship from God can become. God speaks in His Word and His Word corrects, instructs, and directs in His Love. To know what love is and how to attain love in God, you have to seek His Face daily in your life through prayer and praise. If you don't know exactly how to develop your praise for God, just simply read one of the many Psalms King David wrote to God to get you started. Through consistent prayer, the Holy Spirit will give you the words and the behavior to praise the Lord from your spirit man. You must saturate yourself with The Word of God to renew your mind and conform to the Mind of Christ. The Word of God changes your thinking from the carnal man to the spiritual man in that you make more quality decisions especially in relationship choices. The Word of God should be read and heard on a daily basis to change how you used to think, behave, and talk to people. God's Word has healing and restoring power that resurrects the spirit man from his death-like state from housing unclean spirits in the past (**Proverbs 3:8 KJV**). God will give you the revelation and insight in His Word about your particular situation. When you are truly seeking God with all of your might, He will show up on your behalf to move in that situation. Getting the Word within you spirit helps you in your praises, prayer, and purpose in God's Kingdom. Deliverance from strongholds happens when you choose to trust Him to never leave nor forsake when others have in the past (**Hebrews 13:5 KJV**). His love will cover the shame and despair that breaks its hold on you once you realize that God never stop caring for you regardless of what you have been through. True recovery from ungodly soul ties requires you to rid yourself of any distractions which includes people that hinder this process. Remember, temptations will arise and don't think Susie or Bubba won't show up in your life to remember the love you all once shared but you can overcome anything that causes you to do evil with good (**Romans 13:17 KJV**). In the book of James, we are to rejoice in every "trial and proving of your faith bring out endurance and steadfastness and patience" for this builds your character and strengthens your spirit man to become what God wants you to be in life (**James 1:3 KJV**). Satan will continually try to tempt you in the area you were delivered from but you have the Greater One in you to overcome anything or any person that is contrary to what God has for you (**1John 4:4 KJV**). What God has for you is better that what you had in the past especially a soulmate so hold on to what God speaks to you in His Word for this will develop your faith to know better and have better in life.

Your Heart

Out of the heart comes the issues of life and determines your spiritual maturity in God's Kingdom (**Proverbs 4:23 KJV**). Spiritual maturity depends on the conditions of your heart. Ungodly soul ties have put some major heart dents making you feel heartache and heartbreak because of your perceived true love for this person. Much pain has your heart succumb to, that it pumps weakly and cannot endure hardships nor keep you at peace. Your spiritual heart determines the time factor of receiving the Promises of God including a pure, clean vessel. Cleaning your vessel takes purifying your heart to inhabit God's love. The most important thing to begin cleaning your heart is to ask God to purge your spirit and remove anything that's not of God especially when you are fasting and praying. After King David's holy debacle, he asked God to remake his heart and spirit righteous and pure once again. The words used in **Psalms 51: 10-12**, can be a confession to God to help you truly heal your heart from ungodly soul ties (**AMP**). Read the following scriptures and see what God does for your heart:

Amplified Bible Version

Psalms 51:10 Create in me a clean heart, O God, and renew a right, persevering and steadfast spirit within me.

Psalms 51:11 Cast me not away from your presence and take not your Holy Spirit from me.

Psalms 51:12 Restore to me the joy of Your salvation and uphold me with a willing spirit.

God's spirit can heal your heart if He is welcomed and can be effective in ministering to your spirit man for spiritual edification and strength. When you ask God to create in you a clean heart, it takes time for the Holy Spirit to purify your heart for you must release any unforgiveness or resentment that still gives your heart palpitations still. There are people walking around with what is called spiritual palpitations in which their heart is not functioning the way God desires it to because it's still broken in some areas releasing hit or miss blessings from time to time but never a steady continuous flow of blessings. Many believers today walk around with various kinds of heart conditions that keep him or her from having total victory and the abundant life Christ died for us to have (**John10:10 KJV**).

Types of Heart Conditions

God warns us to guard our hearts for it causes the manifestations we see in the physical realm being good or bad. Ungodly soul ties left your heart open to all kinds of negative feelings bombarded by evil spirits constantly, so the issues you have probably stem from the lingering emotions that make you upset easily and sensitive to what people say to you. Offenses affect you greatly since your heart still keeps pumping past hurts within it and to truly heal you have to let it all go to God. You can have such a cold heart that you close people and God out which keeps God from helping you restore your heart to purity. A stony heart blocks the flow of God's love from purification and sanctification. Keeping everything hidden in your heart from God makes the heart remain in an impure state inviting more iniquities to harbor in there. An impure heart doesn't fully have the victory of overcoming challenges in life and more tormenting spirits can invade to attack. Those who possess these tormenting spirits don't have a clean, pure heart and can't combat the attacks because of a weakened heart condition. Eventually, this person may have a heart attack and die spiritually and physically for that matter. God must be allowed to work in your heart to make you spiritually whole in order to reach your full potential in Christ. In order for your heart to become pure and ready for God's Spirit to inhabit fully, it takes the believer to become consecrated to God completely.

Purification, Consecration, and Sanctification

To begin the purification of your heart, it starts with holy living and removing the transgressions out of your life through the guidance of the Holy Spirit. God can change you from within spiritually but there's some physical changes you need to do as well. Purification is certain when you start to remove the sins out of your heart, mind, body, and soul. Sin is anything that can make you act, think, and talk contrary to what Jesus would do. As humans, who walk with the flesh continuously, rebels God's Spirit on a daily basis for sinful gain, our sins can be sometimes unintentional and requires us to be repentant to God each day of our lives. God desires for His People to live free from sins that block His Blessings and end our life prematurely upon this earth. In **1ˢᵗ John 5:18**, John says that "we know [absolutely] that anyone born of God does not [deliberately and knowingly] practice committing sin, but the One Who was begotten of God carefully watches over and protects him [Christ's divine presence within him against the evil], and the wicked one does not lay hold (get a grip) on him or touch [him]" **(AMP).** What you don't want to do is think you have permission to sin all you want to cause you know God will forgive you of all of your sins. Blatant sinning robs you of God's protection and allows The Enemy to bring full assaults in your mind, body, and soul. By the grace of God can we continue to be in God's Presence with our sinful tendencies and have His Blessings in heavenly and earthly places because of His Son, Jesus. But, God expects us to be holy because He is holy meaning sinning isn't a pastime hobby anymore (**1ˢᵗ Peter 1:16 KJV**). The more we sin, the more it grieves the Holy Spirit and causes Him to leave when we need Him to help us to live holy (**Ephesians 4:30 KJV**). Holiness requires you to refrain from sinning to clear out the mess in your heart from past iniquities such as bad relationships. There is also person, places and things you need to cut out of your life in order to overcome your heart issues. Then God can begin to sanctify your temple by helping your spirit man hear The Voice of God for guidance in every decision we make. Once your spirit man becomes clean through consecrated living, the Holy Spirit can begin to develop the fruits of His Spirit so you are a productive vessel in the Kingdom of God living out your divine potential. The Holy Spirit will help you control your fleshly desires by you responding to His unction and wisdom in your everyday living (**Galatians 5:16 KJV**). Once your flesh is under controlled with the Holy Spirit guiding your steps, then the work He produces comes into your spirit and manifests in your vessel such as love, joy, peace, patience, temperance, kindness, goodness, meekness, self-control, and faithfulness (**Galatians 5:22-23 KJV**). If we live by the Holy Spirit, He will continue the process of making your heart strong in the Lord through continuous edification of your spirit man.

Edifying Your Spirit Man

If we live by the Holy Spirit, He will continue the process of making your heart strong in the Lord through continuous edification of your spirit man. The Holy Spirit will help you in prayer by making intercession for you when you don't know quite what to say to God and builds you spiritually up to pray more effectively using The Word of God (**1st Corinthians 14:15 KJV**). The stronger your spirit man becomes, the more pure your heart can be. Prayer has a crucial part in the edification of the spirit man. Building up the spirit man takes communicating with God on a daily basis. Once the spirit man is tuned into God's Spirit then you will be able to hear from God more clearly. Your spirit man will be attuned to discern if this is The Voice of God or The Enemy. Praying in the Spirit by allowing The Holy Spirit to utter words in an unknown tongue helps to build the spirit man up by purging out the flesh's influences in the physical realm. The ability to speak in tongues comes from you asking God to give you the Holy Spirit and yielding your voice for the Holy Spirit to pray God's Perfect Will in your life. Many people in the Body of Christ assume that people who speak in tongues must be holier than thou but that isn't the case. You can be the biggest sinner in the world and speak in tongues. The purpose of speaking in tongues is to enhance and edify your spirit man in prayer. Your prayers will be taken to the next level when you pray in the Spirit in which you are talking directly to God and Satan cannot understand a word of it. The Holy Spirit will help you to pray God's Word more effectively in which it reaches the heavenlies and has power upon the earth. God answers and moves by His Word spoken in the earth that makes your prayers work on your behalf because of the Anointing of God enhancing its power in the earthly realm. The spirit man will yearn to know more of God and seek His Presence through prayer and meditation on His Word. Prayer helps you to develop a more intimate and personal relationships with God who can offer His Wisdom and His Love to you even more so. As you delight yourself in the Lord, He becomes ever so close and personal with you revealing His Most Deepest Thoughts and the blessings He waits to bring into your life. As you edify the spirit man through a consistent prayer life and saturating yourself daily in The Word of God, you have the ability to resist evil and withstand the temptations that will come in your daily walk with God. Each day is a faith fight to keep The Enemy from attacking you by maintaining a holy, consecrated life. That is why it is important to maintain God's whole armour to keep from returning back to your past state of ungodliness and transgression where Satan and people will try to pull you back into **(Ephesians 6:15-17 KJV)**. To keep you spiritually strong in the Lord, you must pray at all times and keeping yourself girded up to live out your destiny in God **(Ephesians 6:18 KJV)**.

Chapter 8: Living Out Your Destiny Free From Ungodly Soul Ties

Are you ready for the God Kind of Life and to embrace what God has for you? Do you have your ticket ready to board the ride of your divine life with God as your pilot to unchartered lands of prosperity living? For once you free yourself from ungodly soul ties, you are ready to run the race living out your divine purpose God has for you. You can now see the truth behind what ungodly soul ties were doing to God's plan in your life and now you can walk in the spiritual and earthly inheritance God has set aside for you to enjoy **(Ephesians 1:3 KJV)**. Now it is time to walk the ordered steps God has already set in place once we get back on the narrow path of righteousness. Satan is truly defeated when you realize how ungodly soul ties were suppose to derail your purpose in life and destroy your life as well. You have now decided to live for God discovering what He has for you to do in the earth. God can guide you into your calling in the Kingdom of God but it's going to take obedience and sacrificing your will to His Will.

Obedience and Sacrifice

Gone are the days where you do whatever you want to do when you are truly living for God. God expects you to be obedient to the spiritual principles found in His Word. His Word helps you to learn how to be obedient to what God tell you to do which demands sacrificing our selfish tendencies. No matter how holier than thou you think you are, living in a fleshly body gives us some fleshly tendencies we battle with on a continual basis. We as people of the Most High are selfish when it comes to being obedient because it hurts the flesh to follow His Word. God's Word instructs man to be obedient so you may eat the good of the land and curses come when you are disobedient to God **(Isaiah 1:19)**. Blessing flood the life of the believer through obedience to God's Way of Living. When we seek His Kingdom and the right way of doing things for God, then all that we desire will surely come to pass **(Matthew 6:33)**. Obedience gets easier when sacrificing our own agenda for God's agenda becomes a top priority in our life.

Putting God First

In every action and decision we make, asking God first on His Wisdom keeps us obedient to His Word and not backsliding into past iniquities. God wants to be the first thing on your mind and who you ask first on anything that concerns you. God should be consulted first in every decision we make that helps us to avoid troubles in our lives when we invite Him to guide us in our daily lifestyles. Also, we must be careful not to seek God first for the sole purpose of getting "The Stuff" and once you get your stuff, God becomes an occasional prayer call when crisis arise in your life. If God is truly the love of your life, the He should be the first thing on your mind as you are blessed to wake up each day. You are blessed to know who God is and how much He cares for you when there are people who wake up not knowing who God is with many troubles on their minds. For those who put God first in their lives, great rewards come from Him by your faithfulness and diligence in wanting to know more of God. In **Hebrews 11:6**, it says that, "But without faith it is impossible to please and be satisfactory to Him. For whoever would come near to God must [necessarily] believe that God exists and that He is the rewarder of those who earnestly and diligently seek Him [out] **(AMP)**. The Great I Am searches the earth for those who strive to know more of Him in order to receive His Power to possess His Promises in the physical realm. Prosperity comes when we seek God in His Word and meditate on the Word to gives us the wisdom to become successful in our ministry and our lives **(Joshua 1:8 KJV)**.

Walking By Faith

Yes, you have decided to follow God's Word being obedient to The Call on your life. By discovering why you are here on this earth, you will find fulfillment in life without the desperate need to involve yourself in another unhealthy, unproductive relationship.

Impatience gets us in trouble when we get weary in waiting on God to change situations in our lives and bring that desired mate we have been praying for **(II Thessalonians 3:13 KJV)**. To fully walk in the love of God and know He has great things in store for use, we must not fall to the traps of The Enemy to get us off focus when the same fool decides to come back for another chance. Let patience bring forth the character development you need in order to be ready to receive your desired mate **(James 1:4 KJV)**. You must believe and trust that God wants what is best for you and His Perfect Will to manifest in due season in your life. There are other things God wants for you to do for ministry in order to truly become a disciple for Christ. He also wants you to prosper in every area of your life maximizing the full potential God has placed in you before your birth **(Jeremiah 1:5 KJV)**. God is going to bless your faithfulness in pursuing His Will in your life and everything The Enemy took from you will be restored in abundance. Faith allows God to truly see how much you trust Him with your needs, wants, and desires. You may desire to be with someone but we need to allow God to develop us spiritually so we can be ready for our future mate. What you truly hope for will come into your life in God's Own Timing. When you did it in your timing, it was wrong and messed your head up which means your matchmaking skills doesn't even compare to God's ability to join two people together. God wants to make sure you love Him and have wholeness in Him before He brings somebody else in the picture. Your love for God should overflow in such abundance that every person you meet should be recipients of that love including your future husband or wife. The things that you need to love are yourself and know that you can't love anybody else until you can love what you see in the mirror.

I Love Me

You love God with your whole being. Eventually, the scars and wounds of ungodly soul ties lose their disheartening stings when you are in the restoration process. By consistently seeking God's Love and His Righteousness, you are discovering the ministry God has placed inside of you. Faith is birthing your trust in God's Way of Living always seeing the desires of your heart manifest once your heart is right towards Him. Your praise is returning to its authenticity after breaking the heavy yokes of ungodly bondages from relationships by releasing the heaviness in your heart. Your spirit man has restored itself to its former glory and you are able to heed the Voice of God to direct your paths. Through prayer, the Holy Spirit is interceding your concerns to God and developing you into the person God already believes you are. What you must make sure to do is love yourself in spite of your faults and flaws that God doesn't see when He talks to you and loves on you. God sees you already in your full divine potential and desires for you to see yourself in the same light. Loving who you are in Christ helps you not to settle for nothing but God's Best in your life. You will love yourself enough not to settle for another ungodly yoked relationship nor allow anyone to make you think you are unworthy of God's Love. The person God has for you will come for the divine purpose of completing The Vision of God for the church before the return of Jesus.

The Abundant Life

Jesus' death gave us the freedom to have life and have it more abundantly **(John 10:10 KJV)**. On your quest to be more Christlike, by not lusting after carnal desire but pursuing what God desires, you must use wisdom to develop godly relationships in terms of friends and a future mate. If they aren't keeping a holy lifestyle then they aren't going to do nothing but corrupt your spirit. Try not to be a scoffer lusting after fleshly desires in order to avoid the judgment of God concerning sexual or perverted vices **(II Peter 3:3 KJV)**. To maintain your holiness and consecration, you can't hang around folks who live in unholy, perverted lifestyles. As children of God, we have the grace of God that is sufficient to handle any temptation in whatever form it comes **(II Corinthians 9:8 KJV)**. In terms of the opposite sex, we will have moments of needing to be with someone to curb the flesh from desiring to have sex with someone. When you are trying to live holy, people enter your life sometimes with not your best interest at heart. Be cautious of the people you associate yourself with so you will not fall into the quicksand of sinful behavior once again. No, you cannot go to the clubs anymore if you are tempted to dance and be with somebody that same night. Don't put yourself in any situation that will compromise your character and vow to live sold out to God. Sexual purity has to involve God giving you the supernatural strength to not fornicate when you really want to. The best way to avoid becoming sexually impure is not to put yourself in situations that compromise your virtues and put you in a vulnerable to relieve your sexual urges. Avoid watching shows that promote unsanctioned sexual relations and make fornication fun to do like recreational sports. Abstaining from sexual sins requires more than just saying no. You have to understand what abstinence is and how important it is not to engage in premarital sex with the one God brings into your life.

To Abstain or Not To Abstain

Church folks not necessarily Christian people tend to preach to the saved and unsaved alike on abstinence. Preaching and not showing people how to abstain from certain activities like sex can be more of a hindrance rather than a solution. We are in such a sexually charged society where sex is available on demand with a multitude advertising encouraging us to please our fleshly desires at every turn. If you were sheltered and not exposed to the world's viewpoint on sex then abstinence may not be as hard for you to do. It all comes down to making a quality decision on the actions you take if you engage in sexual activities and understand the repercussions of your actions. Just saying sex is wrong before marriage in the eyes of God doesn't help a person who has already been committing the act and is trying to curb his or her sexual urges. The problem with abstinence is that many people haven't abstained from the past constantly fighting to keep themselves from sexual sins on a daily basis. Abstinence is hard to teach hormonally challenged teenagers that are exposed to The Enemy's devices of getting them to rebel through pre-marital sex in music, media, and peer influences. It is really hard for those who are trying to be celibate when preachers aren't teaching them how to abstain from fornication when there is temptation everywhere even in the churches. People need to be taught God's Word on what is God's viewpoint on love, sex and marriage so people can realize the importance of waiting on marriage to have sex to avoid ungodly soul ties which accompanies pain, heartache, torment, and possibly death. Also, for a person to have the ability to abstain from participating from sexual activities is to realize that people have a hard time with this because the act of sex is good and pleasurable. The development of ungodly soul ties emerges on the spiritual level first and the spiritual bondage seals and spreads, when he and she engage in the sex act.

God Made Sex Good

Sex is a gift from God created for the marriage bed and not just for recreational purposes like skating and bowling. Sex has been made into a free for all choice activity, whether you are gay or straight used explicitly as a means to achieve optimal pleasures by releasing some stress. Satan utilizes sex as a seductive method of advertising its wonderful attributes in commercials, movies, plays, and music. The Enemy knows that tempting your desire in sex can bring about derailment in your destiny and walk with God. God made sex good to demonstrate an earthly version of the feelings you have when you are truly intimate with Him through a personal relationship. Sex taken out of the equation of marriage may cause lots of pleasurable moans but more torments in the long run when you realize how hard it is to stop once you have went down that road being a Christian too. It is not just the unsaved and untaught who have sex but Christian people as well who think it is cool to do it while preaching a sermon but not being married to the person at all. We call those folks hypocrites who show the unsaved a false way of thinking that God is double-minded because His People act more like the world than like Jesus. It takes repentance and the grace of God to free yourself from the world's way of living the good life meaning being successful, finding a partner, and having lots of sex remaining unmarried so you can have more choices if that person doesn't work out. That is out of the divine order God has set aside for His People concerning sex and marriage. God desires for us to enjoy sex in the proper setting of marriage to have His Protective Covering on it so intimacy becomes even greater between a husband and wife for He is part of the consummation of your wedding vows. The greatest sex you will ever experience is when you allow God to be part of the marriage bed and take it to supernatural levels without the need for special toys, elixirs, gadgets, and gels to make it mind-blowing.

Chapter 9: Preventing Future Ungodly Soul Ties

What About Your Friends?

As you continue your life on the earth until Jesus returns, people will come and go throughout your lifetime for a permanent or temporary season. When it comes to choosing your friends, choose wisely and make sure they are striving for holy living not church living. If you have people presently in your life that are considered to be a friend, ask God to reveal their true intentions towards you to avoid any negative soul ties from occurring. Since we live in an imperfect world with imperfect people, we all have the tendency to pursue our own agendas with hidden motives for selfish reasons unless we are anchored in God. There are people who pretend to be your friend so they can sow worms of discord in your life by betrayal means. Even Jesus had His own backstabber during His Ministry with one of His Own Disciple, Judas, who helped send the Lamb of God to His Death because of his selfish need to have money. Well, Judas' betrayal help to save mankind by the death and resurrection of Jesus, but unless you are Jesus, nothing good can come out of you being friends with a Judas person. When we are friends with fake, jealous folk who put on a godly persona, they will eventually show their true colors by their spiritual fruits. You should know the truth about a person by how fruitful he or she is spiritually that manifests itself into the physical realm. A person's fruitfulness comes from the Holy Spirit working on the inside of them to make him or her into the likeness of Christ. A true friend should be developing their character into Christ-likeness. They shouldn't be bringing forth weeds if they are living truly by the Holy Spirit. Weeds can look green and flourishing like a regular plant but the difference is that they destroy the real greenery appearing to be decorative to the landscape. The friends you think are godly and have your back can have a weed spirit which is anti-Christ in nature in that they will eventually eat away the core of your character, mind, and body to control your destiny and prosperity. A friend with a weed spirit will suck the holiness and godliness out of you making you more like them which can become ungodly soul ties. To prevent ungodly soul ties through friendship, you might have to break off relationships that aren't adding to your walk with God and keeping you from participating in the things of God. As they say, it's for your own good.

My People, God

Cain's actions in the bible towards his brother Abel brought about the first murder and the term dysfunctional family into being. Your family can sometimes be the death of you if you allow ungodly soul ties to form through the spirit of control, spirit of oppression and generational curses. Your family is what The Enemy loves to use to dominate your life through control and curses to hinder the Plan of God from coming to pass in your life destroying the next generation as well. If your family doesn't agree with what God tells you to do, then you pray for them and continue to be obedient to His Will. Not everybody including kinfolk can go where God is taking you nor understand The Call on your life. But the spirit of control can put a halt to your ministry if you allow your family to dictate your life putting you in bondage. Living to please family will put a stronghold on you because you aren't free to please God in every area of your Christian walk. That is when you might have to love your people from a distance to keep your focus on what God instructs you to do. Maybe you are the one God wants to use to break the generational curses in your family. Generational curses come when Satan uses particular spirits to become familiar with the family using their weaknesses, bad habits, and sinful practices. These curses become part of your family lineage in that more familiar spirits latch on to the next generation to continue the cycle of never reaching their full potential in God and truly experiencing the abundant, victorious life. Take a look at how your family lives their life and the events that consistently keep occurring in each generation that constantly cause pain, sickness and death to destroy God's Plan in their lives. God desires to pick a person from the family to create a new lineage of prosperous, anointed people who are truly living a fulfilled life doing their divine purpose in the earth. In the bible, it just took one person to change the whole family line for the better of the next generation who would need someone who would not fall susceptible to generational curses. To save yourself from falling into the trap of your previous generation line, you must ask God to remove the familiar spirits that maybe attacking you from your family and plead the Blood of Jesus to cleanse yourself from these curses. Abraham left his family's home and lifestyle to seek after God's Will and Plan for his Life. When God reveals His Plan for your life, you might have to leave your family behind to save your family being the person who decided that The Enemy will not have free reign to destroy your family anymore through generational curses. Abraham even left his own nephew Lot to continue on his walk with God and was blessed by his faithfulness in what God wanted to do through him to bless the next generation. His decision helped the future with the family lineage he helped to create that eventually became a Royal Priestly Lineage in each generation. The people were obedient to God's Plan in their life and pursued it at all costs that open the doors to a young lady who was from Abraham's lineage that help to bring about the ultimate blessing, Jesus. In each lineage of Abraham, God was able to bring about the many people in the family that He promised Abraham that would be as many as the stars in the sky. In that simple belief that God had his best interest at heart, Abraham helped to bring in the salvation of mankind through Jesus Christ. It is vital to see that your actions will reap its consequences in the next generation and breaking the ungodly soul ties within our family can begin a new family in the Body of Christ and in your own family to spread the gospel of Jesus Christ.

Birthing Your Ministry

To prevent any further ungodly soul ties in the future is to seek the ministry that God has put inside of you from birth to bless His People and save His People from the satanic devices of The Enemy to destroy all of mankind by any means. Your ministry is a constant discovery in finding out what your spiritual gifts are and what you were created to do in the earth to help people come to know Christ before His Return. God will reveal to you in time the full complexity of the Vision He has for you to accomplish in ministry but you have to remain focus on the things He tells you to do. That is why is important to be careful of the friends you keep, the family members you talk to and even some church folks because The Enemy is just looking for a door in those areas to attack you and derail your destiny. Going to church isn't just enough to develop your ministry and if you are not trying to figure out what God wants you to do in your life to bless the Body of Christ. Working in the church is fine and dandy but true ministry starts as soon as you walk out the door and live your everyday life. Coming to church should be an enhancement of your walk with God and the opportunity to bless His People through your spiritual gifts and talents in order to bring others to the knowledge of Jesus for salvation purposes. You are a minister with the spiritual guidance of the Holy Spirit who offers you ideas, instructions, and directions to make sure you are continuing on the righteous path God has already laid out for you before your birth. All you have to do is walk on that path and stay on the path even when The Enemy brings traps and temptations to get you off track. The Holy Spirit is truly a divine part of God that you need in order to develop into the potential God designed you to be birthing out the ministry that is bigger than just you and will affect the world of these times of destructive lifestyles and people living to please themselves and not God.

The Greater One in You

Remember that God's Spirit wants to reside in you completely and help you in every decision of your life but you have to surrender every area of your life to avoid the pitfalls of sinful behavior that can lead to strongholds. God wants to do great things for His People through your vessel and you must strive to keep your vessel clean from soul ties that are detrimental to your ministry in life. In order to become a vessel of truth and honor, you have to be careful in every action and decision you make that affects your spiritual walk with God. The God in you desires for you to have the best in your life and to prosper in the earthly realms in every area of your life.

About the Author

Pastor Demond L.Tolliver is a world-reknown evangelist who travels the world preaching the gospel of Jesus Christ to the lost. He is also the Overseer and Pastor of Bondage Breaking Ministries in Cedar Hill, Texas. God is using him mightily to set the captives free, heal the sick, work miracles, lead people to salvation and be filled with the Holy Ghost. He lives by the mandate of his deliverance ministry which is for every person to experience "a bondage-breaking, yoke destroying, Word from the Lord that will change your life!"